USING URBAN WASTELAND

A GUIDE FOR COMMUNITY GROUPS

SUSAN LOBBENBERG

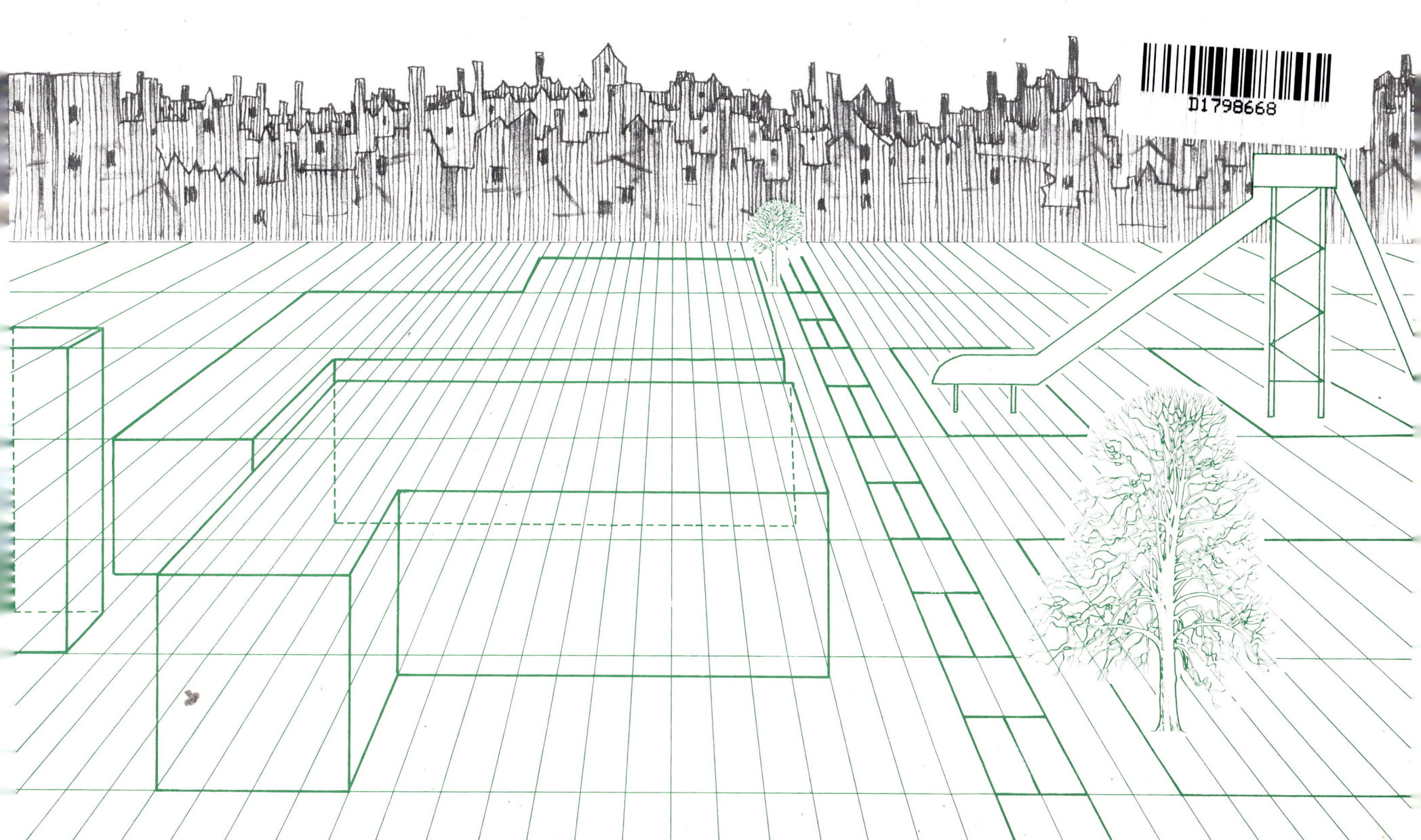

USING URBAN WASTELAND

A ⌐ OUPS

BEDFORD SQUARE PRESS NCVO

First published 1981 by the
BEDFORD SQUARE PRESS of the
National Council for Voluntary Organisations
26 Bedford Square, London WC1B 3HU

ISBN 0 7199 1049 8

Printed in England by Belmont Press, Northampton

A

711
4
L011

83-65133

ii

Contents

1. Where is Urban Wasteland and Why Does It Exist?

Urban changes. Land use. Land values.

2. Government and Local Authority Action on Vacant Inner City Land

Clearance of refuse. The inner cities programme.

3. Voluntary Action on Wasteland

Possible organisations to contact.
Size. Position of the site. Condition of the land.
Who owns the land? The next steps. Finding out the plans for the land.
Planning permission. A licence or lease? Refusal of a licence. Cost.
Conditions of planning permission. Insurance. Some final words of advice.

4. Getting Involved – What Community Groups Can Do

5. Creating Employment from Wasteland Projects

6. Fund Raising

Foreword

'The wind crosses the brown land, unheard.
The nymphs are departed.'
'The Waste Land' by T. S. Eliot

The desolation conjured by Eliot's great poem is a good starting point for reading this book. For the festering holes in our towns and cities are not merely untidy – they disturb the psyche. We can accept that the Sahara and the Arctic cannot be put to much use, but for swathes of inner London and Liverpool to be abandoned and unproductive is an assault on common sense.

The message that we could be using much more of this idle land must be put across again and again and Susan Lobbenberg's concise call to action deserves to be widely read. I particularly welcome her emphasis on what can be done by creative local authorities and voluntary groups.

Her book is timely for it coincides with the new initiatives of the Local Government, Planning and Land Act 1980 which includes measures to bring surplus land forward for re-use. And timely too because it comes at the beginning of the Land Decade declared by the Land Decade Educational Council for the 1980s. The Council aims to increase public awareness about the importance of using our small island's land surface wisely. Avoiding waste is wise even in a profligate society and as we become more appreciative that the earth's resources do not stretch to infinity, so the careful use of all our land grows in significance.

Timothy Cantell

Timothy Cantell was the author of the Civic Trust's report, *Urban Wasteland*. He is now the Assistant Secretary (Environment) at the Royal Society of Arts.

---

1 Wapping Basin, London's East End, 1977.
  With the demise of London's docklands, great tracts of land and water lay empty for decades. Wapping Basin was eventually filled in with rubble and hardcore, and is now being redeveloped.

Illustrations

Introduction

Pockets of vacant and derelict land have become characteristic of inner city areas, creating ugly blemishes on the urban environment and wasting a precious resource.

Awareness of the problem should go hand in glove with action. The last five years have seen an increasing number of local authority schemes to re-use wasteland, but the length of time between recognising the problem and acting on it may vary widely between local authorities.

This book advises community groups and local authorities working on inner city wasteland projects on:
- how and why inner city wasteland has occurred;
- what central and local government is trying to do about it;
- what community groups can do by describing established projects and giving ideas for new ones;
- how to release land for the community;
- how to create employment from wasteland projects; and
- how to finance projects.

Acknowledgements

I should gratefully like to acknowledge the help I received from the following people who have kindly read the text and offered their advice: Rob Cowan and Kelvin Macdonald of the Town and Country Planning Association, Timothy Cantell of the Royal Society of Arts, and Martin Tempia (Wasteland Forum), Robert Davies (Project Development Department) and Richard Grover (Policy Planning) of the National Council for Voluntary Organisations.

Grateful acknowledgement is made to the following for their permission to reproduce photographs:
Piers Carey, no. 5; Free Form, nos. 16, 20, 21; Green Cure Trust, no. 24; Housing Renewal Unit, nos. 6, 7, 8; Inter-Action, nos. 15, 17, 18; Tom Learmonth, nos. 2, 4; Martin Lipson, nos. 1, 3, 9, 10, 11, 14, 19, 22, 23; Merseyside Improved Homes, no. 13; and South Yorkshire County Council, no. 12.

1. Where Is Urban Wasteland and Why Does It Exist?

Where is the urban wasteland?

- Land which cannot be developed because of its inaccessibility, size or the nature of the surrounding developments: for example, land which is near a motorway or railway.
- Private and public land on which the owner has not built.
- Land badly polluted by industrial use.
- Local authority sites with no immediate plans for development: plans might be abandoned because of cut-backs in public expenditure, changes in policy or changes in the property market.
- Land left vacant and derelict by inner city redevelopment: industry moving out, slum clearance and road building.
Disused railways. Timothy Cantell in *Urban Wasteland*[1] estimates that the last sixty-five years have seen the closure of 12,000 miles of railway lines, creating 120,000 acres of vacant land.
Land with buildings which have been prematurely demolished and/or derelict for some years.

Spitalfield's Selby Street site – still waiting for redevelopment.

3 Green Giant site, Vauxhall, London, 1980.
Another prestigious riverfront site lies empty for year after year while developers await their moment. This one caused much controversy with proposals for a 600 foot tower clad in glass, over three times the height of an existing block next door. The Environment Minister 'called in' the application and recommended refusal on aesthetic grounds.
    A similarly overgrown and wasted large site on the other side of Vauxhall Bridge just out of the picture – the 'Effra' site – remained unused for many years, despite being owned by the Department of the Environment. Its new owners are now hoping to get planning permission for a large office development.

4 The clearance of this site in London's Spitalfields began in 1976. It is still derelict.

5 A half-cleared site in Brighton, destined for use as a carpark.
  The demolition was unnecessary, as is the carpark.

6 Derelict land in Liverpool.

Why does urban wasteland exist?

The White Paper *Policy for the Inner Cities*[2] showed that the wide extent of vacant land in inner areas is a major problem:

> . . . the presence of a great amount of vacant under-used or derelict land is one of the most difficult aspects of the inner city situation. It is bound to affect the morale of those who live in the areas and it may well deter prospective developers who tend to see it as evidence of the weakness of economic activity in the areas. Steps to improve the attractiveness of inner area sites and to bring land into use must rank among the urgent tasks of the regeneration of the inner cities. (Para 8, page 27)

The reasons for so much urban wasteland are complex and involve analyses of urban changes since the nineteenth century, of how and why land is used or under-used and of how it is valued. This book only sketches the main causes; for further information see the notes to this chapter and the List of Further Reading.

Urban Changes

Changes in the social and economic fabric of our cities since the late nineteenth century have helped create a depressing phenomenon known as inner city decline. Signs of this decline are apparent in all our inner cities: bleak and desolate townscapes of derelict or poorly maintained houses and industrial buildings; inadequate public transport; a high degree of unemployment and all the poverty and tensions which it generates, and of course, numerous pockets of vacant land, often hidden away by advertisement hoardings or corrugated iron.

Why has it happened? One of the main reasons is that since the 1880s there has been a decentralisation of the population from the inner cities to the suburbs, and since 1946 to the new and expanded towns. For example, Calton, which is part of the Glasgow Eastern Area Renewal Area (GEAR), was the most densely occupied ward in Glasgow in 1871.[3] Yet between 1951 and 1971, the area covered by the GEAR project lost approximately 63,000 people, nearly 37 per cent of its 1951 population. Indeed the population fell further, from 82,000 in 1971 to 45,000 in 1978. In 1976 there were 315 acres of vacant land in the GEAR area. This pattern is a characteristic of all our major cities: between 1961 and 1971 the population of London fell by 13.5 per cent; of Merseyside by 17.0 per cent and of south-east Lancashire by 16.0 per cent.[4] Such an exodus was clearly linked to people's desire to move from the inner city slums (as Ebenezer Howard said in 1899,[5] from the 'foul air, high rents and fogs'), and to more contemporary industrial and employment changes in inner city areas.

The last twenty years have seen a great number of firms closing down in our cities, especially manufacturing firms. In South-east London, between 1964 and 1974, there were 231 closures of manufacturing firms with a total employment of 39,000 and 20 openings with a total employment of 894 (Department of Industry data). Such closures, or outmigration of firms, are caused by capital restructuring, by government regional policies and by local authorities' redevelopment plans. Population decentralisation leads to a reduction in the labour supply, which produces labour shortages. Firms move out, resulting in a loss of employment opportunities, so workers move likewise. Expanding firms are encouraged to move out of inner cities by government regional policies of industrial relocation, attracting industry to new and expanded towns, or by local authorities' redevelopment plans. Improved communications and transportation have also enabled firms to move out of the inner city, since they no longer have to rely on central specialist services. As employers, employees and capital investment move from the inner city to outer

7 The Carlisle and Cumberland Road area in Portsmouth. A classic case of 'prior demolition', where the council demolished houses and blighted the area as a tactical means of 'bulldozing' the opposition to a road scheme for which the plans had not yet been approved. Often in such cases the redevelopment plans fall through, and the site remains derelict.

8 Derelict back court in Govan, Glasgow.
  Many such courts are now being improved by community-
  based housing associations.

areas, so land demand is reduced, leaving acres of vacant inner city sites.

Lastly, there has been an enormous amount of physical change in inner cities, resulting in vacant land, because of slum clearance and redevelopment. Major slum clearance began with the Housing Act of 1930, but the first real slum drive started in 1933, and by 1939, 266,000 dwellings had been demolished in Britain. Following a lull between the two World Wars, the slum clearance programme was pursued vigorously until the early 1970s. For example, 15,600 dwellings were demolished in the inner areas of Liverpool between 1966 and 1969, with only 3,800 dwellings built on the cleared land. The Final Report of the Liverpool Inner Area Study (1977) stated: 'In 1975, 11 per cent of the land in the study area was lying vacant, much of it in the cleared sites of terraced houses.' However, slum clearance is now no longer a significant cause of vacant land, since local authorities either improve housing rather than demolish it or try to ensure that redevelopment quickly follows clearance.

Land Use

The use or non-use of land is decided by who owns it; the vagaries of the property market which determine how the land is valued; future plans for it; when and whether these plans are implemented; and when and whether it is bought or sold.

A recent survey of the ownership of vacant urban sites, *Urban Wasteland* by the Civic Trust,[6] estimates that: '. . . of the 279 plots, a third were in the ownership of the county or district council, a regional council in Scotland, or a London Borough Council . . . public organisations accounted for 45 per cent of the dormant sites and private firms, individuals, churches, estates and trusts 40 per cent'.

9 Gas Board land, Tower Hamlets, London, 1980.
Years of blight destroyed a once friendly community near these gasworks. An open space, planned by the council to replace these unfit homes, is perfectly sited across a busy main road from the run-down council estate, and under the shadow of the gasworks. To make matters worse the grinding, piecemeal demolition of the terraces has left families living amidst uncleared rubble, rats and continuous dumping.

Privately owned vacant land in inner cities tends to fall into a number of categories. A recent survey of vacant land in Wandsworth found that 70 per cent of privately owned vacant land was owned by property companies, local builders and local firms; 11 per cent was owned by commercial undertakings such as retailers; 8 per cent was owned by private individuals; 7 per cent was owned by religious organisations and 4 per cent was owned by individual firms. Of publicly owned vacant land: 33.6 per cent was owned by British Rail; 31.8 per cent by the Post Office; 9.6 per cent by the Central Electricity Generating Board and London Electricity Board and the rest was owned by London Transport Executive, Thames Water, HMSO and the Home Office. In general, inner city land holdings tend to be in fragmented ownership.

The lack of development and subsequent abandonment of many publicly and privately owned sites can be partly attributed to property boom induced speculation. Many sites owned by property companies in inner London boroughs were bought in the property boom of 1972-74. When property prices fell in the mid-70s and developers found their plans no longer viable, they were reluctant to cut their losses and sell their sites. And since it was not financially viable to develop the land, it remained vacant whilst appreciating in value. Development risks are, in any case, often greater in the inner city.

Both private and public developers tend to retain 'redundant' land for future use, in particular sites which already have planning permission and access to strategic services such as railway lines. So even if the site is no longer being used and its future use is uncertain, there is a strong incentive to simply retain the land rather than dispose of it. Indeed, Northern Developments, a property developer, held over 10,000 sites with outline planning permission for residential zoning.[7] Private and public owners are also frequently reticent to allow sites to be made available for temporary non-commercial use (see chapter 3) because of the possible future

difficulties of regaining possession of the land. The subsequent construction delays and legal costs are seen as prohibitively high, compared to the cost of the land remaining vacant.

A further reason for empty undeveloped sites is the cessation of such uses as mineral extraction, agriculture or allotments. Furthermore, the land may be contaminated by pollutants or kept vacant because of hidden construction hazards such as cellars.

Planning delays are a contributory factor to urban wasteland. They have helped create a phenomenon known as 'planning blight'. Plans for residential, industrial or recreational land use, within the local authority's Development Plans, are frequently subject to long delays between implementation and completion. The delays may be due to a number of factors such as lengthy negotiations over detailed planning applications and disagreements over schemes between local authority departments or the local authority and a private developer. The National Building Agency[8] calculates that the average time for a site to be developed from outline planning application to completing the construction of a new housing development is 7.5 years, compared with an average total time of 2.8 years for a development without planning delays.

Indeed, planning delays and financial restraints may also affect comprehensive redevelopment schemes, leaving their stamp of large-scale urban dereliction. The starting dates of schemes may be postponed or there may be a long time before the plans are implemented – following a public inquiry or the result of the Secretary of State's decision on the confirmation of a Compulsory Purchase Order. It has been calculated that the average time for this process is at least two years.[9]

Financial cutbacks have also helped create inner city wasteland. Reductions in local authorities' finances result in them being unable to buy land for development or to finance schemes. Strathclyde Regional Council explained that:[10]

The existence of extensive areas of vacant land should not be taken as an indication of lack of planning proposals, but rather as an inability to implement these proposals due to difficulties of finance, manpower, and statutory procedural requirements. In addition, some sites in the Central Area are derelict because of the current depressed state of the commercial property market.

Land Values
Land values play a contributory part in keeping inner city land vacant. Prohibitively high land values make it difficult for local authorities and nationalised industries to acquire land for development. They also create a disincentive for disposing of vacant land.[11]

The value of land is the price it will reach in the open market. This price is determined by a host of demand and supply factors, the most important of which are the type of development which is allowed on the land, its location and the buildings already on it. The practice of putting a value on land or buildings is part science and part guesswork. This book will only touch on some of the major issues.

In practice, most land values are not based upon sales but on the expectation of value if the land were to be sold under specified conditions. For example, a farmer will want a higher value for land he hopes can be sold for housing than for land committed to agriculture. A developer will place a high value on an old industrial site on which he hopes to get permission for offices. All over cities and towns there are 'hope values' based upon assumptions of future use. If all these sites were to be put on the market at one time, of course, the market would collapse exposing the falseness of these values.

The value of land does not therefore tell us much about what is taking place on land. Derelict land can be valued at far more than housing estates or industrial areas. A run-down shopping parade can cost more than a large factory site. A rough rule of thumb is that the value is

10 Coin Street, South Bank, London, 1980.
Coin Street is the site of a classic local planning struggle elevated to a national challenge to the public inquiry system. This key inner city area, comprising several distinct parcels of land, lies alongside the Thames, the National Theatre and a deliberately run-down industrially-based residential area. The community fought hard for homes and new life on the site, against multi-national developers keen to build offices. A long inquiry did not resolve the battle, but it did open up a serious question about the validity of local plans.

1 Wandsworth Gas Works site, London, 1980.
Families of travellers stay for a few weeks at a time on sites all over the country which have become scrap-heaps. These travellers are of Welsh origin and were living on the old . gasworks site, scratching a temporary living from old iron. They had heard rumours that the site contained highly toxic chemicals and were concerned, not so much for their own 'canny' children as for those from local estates. The GLC, owners of this very large site, had neglected fences and security; the travellers permitted this photograph to be used to help get the fences put up. One week after it was taken, a local boy of ten was drowned in a highly polluted gas holder base easily accessible from the perimeter road. This site is now fenced, just as dangerous and without definite plans for use, in an area with a housing shortage and high unemployment.

proportional to the rent either flowing from the site or an expectation of a rent. Since office rents are higher than industrial rents and both are higher than the rent of farm land, a rough idea of the hierarchy of land values can be gained.

One reason why the value of land does not reflect the activity taking place on it is that the minimum value land can have is its 'existing use value'. The existing use means the 'zoned use', not its current condition. For example, a derelict factory can have as great a value as a factory which is fully operational. A prime case of this recently was a value of £10 million placed on the disused factory and offices of the Morgan Crucible premises in Battersea, London. This was far higher than the value of the land as residential – around £2 million – and prevented the local council receiving loan sanction for compulsory purchase as a housing site. The value was thus based on the existing use and not the intended use. Existing use values keep up the price of property in run-down areas and are the reason why some people have been arguing that the base for valuation should be 'current use value' or the value of the activity actually on the site. This would substantially reduce the price of derelict land.

The Royal Town Planning Institute (RTPI) in their report *Land Values and Planning in the Inner Areas*[1][2] identify different types of land market-areas of the country that are experiencing different demands for property and patterns of land value. These are:

● Where land is very expensive because high value uses such as offices or hotels are bidding for it. Hope values are spread over quite a large area. This is common in and around the central areas of cities and towns and accounts for the conflict over land at places like Coin Street and Covent Garden in London. Socially necessary uses are squeezed out slowly by demand for high value uses.

● Where there is little demand for land with values reflecting redundant uses such as warehouses, docks or railway yards. Often the cost of land clearance and preparation will be higher than the land value.

These are the extreme cases but within any town or part of a city elements of the two can be found. Areas of publicly owned land are special cases where values will be complicated by uses such as parks, schools and hospitals. There is considerable debate about what value if any this land should have. There is as yet no basis for assessing the social value of land.

2. Government and Local Authority Action on Vacant Inner City Land

Government action

The spread of vacant land in inner urban areas has only recently been perceived by the government as a problem. Indeed, this factor could be seen as contributing to the extent of urban wasteland. However, there have been various recent initiatives which will help local authorities and community groups take action:

● In September 1979, the Secretary of State for the Environment, Michael Heseltine, announced his decision to set up a public register of wasteland owned by local government and other public bodies. This is provided by Part X of the Local Government Planning and Land Act 1980 which was passed by Parliament in November 1980. The aim is to encourage a speedy resale of derelict land and to give the Secretary of State powers to order land sales on the open market.

Once a local authority area has been named, the following bodies currently have a duty to notify the Secretary of State of any vacant land holdings in that area:*

(1) County councils, district and London borough councils, the GLC, the Common Council of the City of London, New Town Development Corporations, the Commission for the New Towns and Urban Development Corporations.
(2) Statutory undertakers as defined in S.290 of the Town and Country Planning Act 1971, the British Airports Authority, the Civil Aviation Authority, the National Coal Board, the Post Office, the Housing Corporation, British

Shipbuilders, the British Steel Corporation and any other authority, body or undertakers which by virtue of any enactment are to be treated as statutory undertakers for any of the purposes of the 1971 Act.
(3) Any other authority, body or undertakers specified in any order made by the Secretary of State, including Crown Land.

While the Registers are to be compiled by the Secretary of State, they will be open to inspection during working hours and on payment of fee, at the offices of the local district council or London borough. If it appeared to the Secretary of State for the Environment, acting jointly with the appropriate sponsoring Minister, that land owned by the public sector was not being used, he could direct that it be offered for sale. The owner would receive market value and would be allowed reasonable time to establish a use for the land. (See the Local Government, Planning and Land Act 1980, ss. 93-100.)

● Derelict land grants are available to private individuals, public bodies and local authorities, through an amendment of provisions within the Local Government Act 1966. Grants are available for land 'which is derelict, neglected or unsightly, requiring reclamation or improvement', and for 'purposes connected with the reclamation or improvement of land'. Grants are also available for land which is 'liable to become derelict, neglected or unsightly by reason of actual or apprehended collapse of the surface as a result of the carrying out of underground mining operations' other than those connected with working or getting coal (Local Government, Planning and Land Act 1980, s. 117).

The Act extends the direct payment of grants to private individuals for the first time; community groups may therefore apply for grants for their projects on derelict sites.
The Act includes a provision enabling grants to be paid towards the cost of surveys and investigations of derelict land, whether or not an approved scheme of reclamation is eventually carried out. Grants will also be paid towards the cost of providing development infrastructure including basic services such as sewers and access roads.

● The White Paper *Policy for the Inner Cities* (Cmnd 6845, June 1977) observed that: 'Much can be done temporarily to put land to use, to landscape it, to grass over ugly sites, through a policy of positive land management.' It also indicated that voluntary groups working with local authorities have an important role in rejuvenating inner city areas – including work on wasteland:

Some things are better done, or done more satisfyingly if they are undertaken by voluntary groups and bodies. The improvement of the inner areas needs to harness the good will and energies of tenants' and residents' associations, local councils of social service, settlements and charities, and more informal groups such as pensioners' clubs. Public policy should aim to stimulate voluntary effort and help voluntary bodies play a constructive role. (Part IV, para 35)

More recently, government policy towards who develops wasteland has broadened. The Secretary of State, Mr Heseltine, said at the Institution of Municipal Engineers' seminar on derelict land, in February 1980:

What we want is to make the development of derelict urban sites a more attractive proposition for local authorities and private developers . . . spending on reclamation this year will be about £23.5m and I would hope to be able at least to maintain it at this level

---

*See 'Wasteland Discussion Document' produced by the Wasteland Forum, National Council for Voluntary Organisations (NCVO), 1981.

next year. What the new powers will do, immediately they come into effect [the land register, derelict land grant, Urban Development Corporations and Enterprise Zones], is to enable us to grant-aid a wider range of schemes including some on difficult or expensive sites not previously attempted.

- The Inner Urban Areas Act (1978) empowered the Secretary of State to designate any district 'if he is satisfied that special social need exists in any inner urban area, and that the conditions which gave rise to the existence of that need could be alleviated by the exercise of the powers conferred by the Act' (Inner Urban Areas Act 1978).* The designated districts include the inner city partnership and programme authorities and a number of other inner city authorities (see pp. 15-16).

Under the Act district and county authorities can undertake the following action in designated districts:
- They can make loans at commercial rates for land purchase and works on land up to 90 per cent of the value of the land and buildings, regardless of whether the authority owns the land.
- They can establish Improvement Areas where grants and loans may be paid for environmental improvements or to improve and convert buildings to be used for industrial and commercial purposes.
- They can make loans or grants to enable them to establish a common ownership or co-operative enterprise.

District and county authorities in partnership areas which are designated districts can be made into Special Areas, by order of the Secretary of State, to:

- make interest-free loans for up to two years, for site preparation works, installation of services and provision of access roads;
- make grants to assist with the rent of commercial and industrial buildings;
- make grants to small firms towards the interest payable on loans for the acquisition of land or carrying out works on that land.

- The Secretary of State has asked local authorities to dispose of surplus land at the best market price 'reasonably' obtainable rather than not selling in order to accumulate interest, or selling at a very high rate.

- He has also asked nationalised industries and statutory undertakers to review vacant and under-used land holdings in partnership areas.

- 'Operation Clean Up' was a government initiative launched in September 1978, which aimed to improve the visual environment of the twenty-nine inner city districts in the partnership and programme areas. It included a range of small projects initiated by local authorities or voluntary groups to improve wasteland, streets and derelict buildings. The remaining funds for the scheme were subsumed by the Urban Programme allocations. Some authorities still fund similar projects.

- Funds from the Urban Programme are available for projects run by both local authorities and voluntary organisations (for which central government pays 75 per cent of approved expenditure). The Programme now takes two forms. First, the 'Traditional' Urban Programme which is available for local authorities throughout England and Wales which have evidence of 'special social need', other than those authorities with special inner city partnership or programme authority status. Applications are invited from local authorities on an annual basis in response to a Department of Environment (DOE) Circular. Capital, non-capital and small-scale holiday projects are eligible if they are within the

criteria and below the upper expenditure limits (in 1981/82 the upper limits were £140,000 for capital and £40,000 for revenue). Special emphasis is given to voluntary and community self-help projects, and in these cases the local authority must pay 25 per cent of the sum applied for. Secondly, there are block allocations of Urban Programme funds made to inner city partnership and progamme authorities in respect of their Inner Area Programmes. Voluntary organisations have benefited extensively from this part of the programme, which now has a bias towards environmental and economic projects, as well as towards cost-effective projects run by voluntary groups.*

- The government has set up Urban Development Corporations in London's Docklands and Merseyside, to secure the regeneration and development of these areas. The Local Government, Planning and Land Act 1980, ss. 134-172, explains the powers of these Corporations:
    . . . bringing land and buildings into effective use, encouraging the development of existing and new industry and commerce, creating an attractive environment and ensuring that housing and social facilities are available to encourage people to live and work in the area.
They are enabled to acquire land (by agreement or compulsorily), within or adjacent to an urban development area or which they require for the provision of services. They are also enabled to dispose of any land as they 'consider expedient for securing the regeneration of the corporation's area or for purposes connected with the regeneration of the area'.

- In April 1980 the government announced its intention to set up Enterprise Zones. The aim is to encourage industrial and commercial

---

*See 'Inner Urban Areas Act 1978: Explanatory note for voluntary organisations', produced by the Inner Cities Unit, NCVO.

*Guidelines for voluntary organisations are published by the NCVO Inner Cities Unit.

development in areas of up to 500 acres, suffering severe decay and deprivation. Benefits for development include exemption from Development Land Tax; 100 per cent capital allowances for industrial and commercial buildings; 100 per cent derating of industrial and commercial property; a simplified planning control system with the Secretary of State agreeing with the local planning authority the broad planning proposals and policies for the area and the arrangements for ensuring quick decisions. Within the overall aim of stimulating industrial and commercial activity, the government sees Enterprise Zones as tools for helping ensure that unused urban land gets back into productive use.
- Finally, there are various powers available under Planning and Housing Acts which apply to vacant land.

The *Town and Country Planning Act 1971,* Section 60 enables orders for the preservation of trees and woodlands to be made by local authorities.
Section 65 authorises local authorities to serve a notice to the owner and occupier of any vacant site, open land or garden whose condition seriously injures the amenity of the area, requiring them to take steps to abate the injury. Section 277 (as amended by the Town and Country Amenities Act 1974) gives powers to designate areas which have special architectural or historic interest, the character of which it is desirable to preserve or enhance, as a conservation area. Grants may be available in these cases by recommendation of the Historic Buildings Council.

The *National Parks and Access to the Countryside Act 1949* (as amended by the Local Government Act 1972) enables the establishment of local nature reserves.

The *Housing Act 1969* (Part 2) gives authority to declare a General Improvement Area in which the amenities of predominantly residential areas can be improved at the same time as the housing.

The *Housing Act 1974* (Part 4), which implements Housing Action Areas, also has implications for environmental improvements including wasteland. Grants are available to local authorities in both these cases.

Clearance of Refuse
Certain legislation is also available under the Public Health and Refuse Disposal Acts which can be used in connection with wasteland sites.

The *Public Health Act 1936* (Part 3) authorises the serving of an abatement notice to clear 'any accumulation or deposit which is prejudicial to health or is a nuisance'.

The *Public Health Act 1961* gives powers to local authorities to remove any rubbish which is seriously detrimental to the amenities of the neighbourhood and to provide and maintain in any street or public place receptacles for refuse or litter.

The *Control of Pollution Act 1974,* Section 22 instructs local authorities to clear highways in the interest of public health or the amenities of the area.

The *Refuse Disposal (Amenity) Act 1978* authorises the removal of motor vehicles appearing to be abandoned on a highway (Section 3) and the removal of other refuse on any land forming part of a highway (Section 6).

For further information about central government action on wasteland, contact the *Department of Environment, 2 Marsham Street, London SW1P 3EB. Tel: 01-212 3434.*

The Inner Cities Programme
Although the Urban Programme has been in existence since 1968, present inner city policies stem from the White Paper, *Policy for the Inner Cities* (Cmnd 6845, June 1977). This provides for:
- The selective designation of those inner city areas with the most severe problems to receive special resources and powers. There are 6 Partnership Areas, 15 Programme Areas and 14 other districts in England with industrial and economic powers under the Inner Urban Areas Act 1978.
- The creation of a special partnership between central and local government, the voluntary sector and local communities to work together in tackling the social, economic and environmental problems of urban areas. Partnership and Programmes Areas would be required annually to draw up frameworks for action documents or Inner Area Programmes.
- Greatly increased Urban Programme resources in the form of block allocations.

Despite the change of government in May 1979, the programme has been retained although a number of changes have been made. There is now greater stress on the economy, the environment and the involvement of the private sector, and on streamlining the administrative machinery.
As mentioned earlier, the Local Government, Planning and Land Act 1980 makes provision for the establishment of Urban Development Corporations. They have powers of planning, land assembly, industrial and commercial development (see p. 14).

Areas in the Inner Cities Programme in England

Inner City Partnership Authorities	Inner City Programme Authorities
Birmingham	Bolton
Hackney and Islington	Bradford
Lambeth	Hammersmith
Liverpool	Hull
Manchester and Salford	Leeds
	Leicester

Inner City
Partnership Authorities
Newcastle and
   Gateshead

Inner City
Programme Authorities
Middlesbrough
North Tyneside
Nottingham
Oldham
Sheffield
South Tyneside
Sunderland
Wolverhampton
Wirral

In addition the following districts, together with their respective county councils, are designated under the Inner Urban Areas Act 1978:
Barnsley
Blackburn
Brent
Doncaster
Ealing
Haringey
Hartlepool
Rochdale
Rotherham
St Helens
Sandwell
Sefton
Wandsworth
Wigan

Local authority action

Despite growing awareness of the large extent of inner area wasteland, local authorities have generally not acted speedily towards finding practical solutions. However, there are some notable exceptions, which may help prompt other authorities into action.

- The Inner Area Studies group examined vacant land within the Toxteth, Wavertree and Edge Hill areas of Liverpool, in 1975. They found that 138 acres (part of a total of 1,257 acres) were vacant, and of this, only 6 per cent had been landscaped and maintained. They also found that 75 per cent of this wasteland was owned by Liverpool City Council, and 50 per cent of it had been empty for at least two years.[1]

- The London Borough of Southwark publishes an annual list of *Vacant and Potentially Vacant Sites* throughout the Borough. The sites are plotted on an ordnance survey map,[2] and are distinctively marked as London Borough of Southwark-owned, GLC-owned and privately owned.

- Other Inner London boroughs have written reports on vacant land, based on their own surveys and research. The London Borough of Lambeth has published a *Vacant Land Survey within the Borough;*[3] the London Borough of Tower Hamlets has published *Vacant Land in Tower Hamlets,*[4] and has made a detailed study of vacant land in Spitalfields, which shows that twenty-six acres of Spitalfields was vacant and derelict or leased out for some temporary use in 1976. The *Spitalfields Housing and Planning Rights Service, Spitalfields Centre, 192 Hanbury Street, London E1 5HO, tel: 01-247 2964,* can give further, up-to-date information on vacant land in the area.

- Local authorities outside London are slowly working on reducing the amount of urban wasteland and concomitant derelict buildings. Birmingham, Nottingham and Newcastle have published details of their total land holdings, which can be obtained through their Planning Departments.

- Some councils have concentrated on problems resulting from vacant land, such as vandalism. Halton Borough Council had a very effective anti-vandalism campaign in 1976/7, encouraging people to undertake environmental improvements themselves, with the help of grant aid and support of the Council.[5]

- South Yorkshire County Council's Environment Department has been helping community groups working on environmental improvement projects since 1975.* The County Council identifies sites from its designated Improvement Priority Areas. Many sites are large, although the Department stresses that it gives equal weight to small scale sites.

  The County Council contacts owners of the sites and carries out all the technical work such as getting a licence and design work, whilst volunteers carry out physical work such as site preparation, grassing, tree planting and paving. A liaison officer acts as a 'link man' between the County Council and local groups. The Council administers a tool bank, which loans spades, rakes, wheelbarrows, etc. to parish councils, schools and community groups. It also encourages people to tidy up sites by hiring skips. However, the more difficult sites are solely worked on by direct labour organisations.

- A recent initiative by Hackney Borough Council and a local umbrella group, Hackney Community Action, points the way to further local authority involvement with community groups wanting to improve vacant inner city

---

* A general overview of the Council's environmental improvement work with local groups is contained in their magazine *Contact*. Back issues can be obtained from the Environment Department, South Yorkshire County Council Regent Street, Barnsley, South Yorkshire.

sites. The Borough has identified 212 vacant sites, covering over 95 areas where 60 per cent of the sites are owned by statutory authorities.

The Council has approved a standard licence which gives community groups the right to use vacant sites for projects such as allotments and play areas, until development actually takes place. The Council will also make up to £500 available for each of the sites where a plan is presented and approved. The money may be spent on site clearance, plants and trees, fencing and garden furniture amongst other uses. Information and advice on finding the site owner, on plans for the area and possible temporary uses for the site can be obtained from the *Planning Department, Hackney Borough Council, Town Hall, Mare Street, London E8 1EA* and *Hackney Community Action, 380 Old Street, London EC1V 9LS.*

● The Planning and Transportation Committee of the Association of Metropolitan Authorities published a report on the *Development of Publicly Owned Urban Land* (September 1979).* They included the following recommendations:

Records of void and under-occupied land and property should be held by all public sector bodies. The information should be formally reported to an appropriate service committee or board along with a progress report briefly showing land and property brought back into use each year.

Information systems should be adequate but . not elaborate. The objective is to bring void and under-occupied land into a viable or socially appropriate use as rapidly as possible and not to create organisations costly to maintain and which can provide answers to questions rarely likely to be asked.

The public sector should be required to justify

the retention of land held for projects not included in approved programmes and under-developed land or property before an independent adjudicator.

Planning authorities must regularly review land use allocations in relation to the real world which allows for constraints on local authority expenditure and the general supply/demand position in the market.

Land and property should be released at the price that it will command in the market provided that there is certainty that development will take place irrespective of any historic acquisition costs or an inspired guess that a better price might be obtained tomorrow. The need is to secure successful disposal today to achieve viable forms of development that will result in new job opportunities, new homes and increased economic activity.

The speedier release of public land for use by local authorities should be facilitated by agreements that will provide for the legal estate to be transferred and possession taken as if a compulsory purchase order had been confirmed and a vesting declaration made with provision for the measure of compensation to be determined by the Lands Tribunal. The development of public sector land should in no sense be frustrated by virtue of delays in the transfer of a legal interest or the assessment of compensation.

The real aim must always be to ensure that land and property is brought into optimum use and not merely transferred from the ownership of the public sector to the private sector or from one element of the public sector to another and left vacant and idle.

Available from the Association of Metropolitan Authorities, 36 Old Queen Street, London SW1H 9JE.

12 Clearing a site at Rawmarsh, north of Rotherham, one of the first urban small sites to be tackled by volunteers.

13 Local children help clear a derelict builders' yard at Monfa Road on Merseyside. The site had been boarded up with corrugated iron for years and had been an eyesore in an area lacking open space. It has now been laid out as a public garden and is managed and maintained by the local residents' association.

3. Voluntary Action on Wasteland

Since relatively little practical help to transform patches of vacant and derelict land is forthcoming from the government or local authorities, the best strategy is for a community group to work and campaign for the use of wasteland. This can both benefit the environment and generate community spirit and co-operation.

Forming a group[1]

In many cases there may already be a group in the locality – a tenants' association, local Friends of the Earth, or amenity group, for example – who can take on a project. However, much work is entailed if the group has to be formed from scratch. Indeed, the nature of the group formed will clearly relate to the land and project – there may be some who have a site and others who have a project but no site. Talk to neighbours, friends and any others about the idea of forming a group. It will help if you have a name for it, a proper constitution and if you can demonstrate that you are a responsible body.

Possible organisations to contact
Wasteland Forum*
Friends of the Earth*
Inter-Action*
Youth groups
Young political groups
Rotary club
Church and women's groups
Play organisations
Local schools which might be interested in helping with a project
Local newspapers

*See the Appendix for the address.

The Site

Various considerations will influence the choice of a site. Ask the local planning authority if it has a map of vacant land in the area. If not, either make a survey (contact the local planning department for help) or choose a site which is an obvious eyesore and which has already attracted public attention.

When assessing the site, groups should bear in mind what they want to make out of it. For example, it could be used for recreational or horticultural projects (see chapter 4).

Size
It is important to relate the size of the site to the type of project envisaged, the size of the group and the amount of support it has. There is no optimum size, although the larger the site, the more work and time will be entailed.

Position of the site
Find out if the site is near sources of industrial pollution; what sort of access there is to it; whether the site is threatened by changes in the water level, etc. Contact your local planning department or the *Planning Aid Unit* at the *Town and Country Planning Association (TCPA), 17 Carlton House Terrace, London SW1Y 5AS. Tel: 01-930 8903.* The Unit gives free planning advice and information to community groups and individuals. Consider the neighbours' reactions— it is always helpful to have them as allies!

Condition of the land
Appearance may not determine the usability of the land. If it looks completely overgrown and full of rubbish, the local authority can clear it away. Check whether the land has been contaminated; the environmental health officer in your locality will advise groups.

As yet there is no national land use survey. However, Dr Alice Coleman of the University of London is currently doing research into the extent of derelict and underused land in Britain, in the Second Land Utilisation Survey.
The *Land Decade* is also doing research and campaigning for the better use of land. They can be contacted at the *Land Council, 9 Queen Anne's Gate, London SW1H 9BU. Tel: 01-222 4333.*

Releasing the land for the community

Who owns the land?
Find out the name of the owner.† Although owners of property do not have to disclose names within our legal system, their names often exist on record in the Land Registry, if the land is registered. (Contact *HM Land Registry, 32 Lincoln's Inn Fields, London WC2A 3PH. Tel: 01-405 3488.*)

The simplest thing is to look at the site and see if there are any estate agents' hoardings on it. They might disclose the owner's name, but they are not legally obliged to do so.

If the property is privately owned but is not for sale through an estate agent, find out who owns it by asking neighbouring tenants, residents or workers. The police or fire brigade may know something, or the local press may be interested enough to find the owner.

Finally, the borough treasurer (or director of finance) will often agree to forward a letter to the owner or leaseholder for you.

The property may be publicly owned by the council or a Port Authority or some other statutory agency who have to say if they own it. If

---

† See Ed Berman's 'Playing the (Wasteland) Game', Inter-Action, 1978 (unpublished). Available from Inter-Action. This details some of the procedures for releasing land.

the land is next to publicly owned land such as a railway goods yard, ring the British Rail Property Board (Regional Division) and ask who it belongs to. Inter-Action Advisory Service could act as your 'agent' in relation to British Rail wasteland enquiries. Even if the land does not belong to the body you have approached, they may know who does own it. Ring the council's valuation office and ask which department/committee owns the land. Remember that with local government reorganisation, there are several levels of government (district/metropolitan/county), who may own the property. Probably the best way is to ask your local councillor for help, if the officials cannot do so quickly enough.

The next steps
Approach the owners, the council representative, the British Rail Property Board if it is British Rail land, the estate agent or the private owner and ask at least four questions:

● Is the land available? If not, could it not be made available under contract to return it on demand and not to build on it?

● If it is available, for how long in the first instance? Try to get as long a period as possible. Less than a year might be a waste of time, depending on how much work is needed.

● Are there any restrictions on, or problems with the property?

● Would the owners consider letting a group use it on a temporary basis for a peppercorn rent? This is a small amount, such as one pound, which validates the transaction.

---

14 Morgan Crucible site, Battersea, London, 1979.
Members of a local action group are here seen creating a people's park out of a site adjoining a big derelict factory. The group was drawing attention to the need for open space, and to the refusal of the GLC (owners of the site) to use it as a bargaining weapon to ensure that developers provided a replacement open space. Behind the hoarding stood the famous Battersea mural demolished by stealth at the hands of the frightened speculators.

Finding out the plans for the land
Having discovered the owner, find out what the permitted planning use of the property is – i.e. has the land been designated for commercial, housing, industrial or some other use. Ask the planning department: telephone or write to them with a specific description of the property. A map with a line around the area in question will help.

Planning permission
At some point before buying or leasing, it must be established whether the plans for the property will be accepted by the planning committee. This is a simple procedure of submitting a planning application by completing a short form from the planning department. In most cases attach to this a drawing or map of the site with a line around the relevant area.

It is the law, clearly marked on each form, that the planning department *must* reply within a statutory number of days.

For buildings or any property that is more than temporary, detailed planning approval will be needed later. Such approval requires completion of another form and detailed drawings and specifications.

There is a charge for submitting a planning application.* This charge varies with the nature of the proposed development but for small-scale projects will most likely be £20-£40.

The planning department can act as consultants: they will offer advice on matters such as parking, access to roads and safety in road crossings, which will be included in the planning application. The planning committee will want to see that you have considered such issues when looking at your application.

Remember that both new and renovated buildings have to be inspected to check that they conform to building regulations. Contact the building inspector or the district surveyor (within the inner London area). Also, contact the fire officer about fire regulations and check the following: refuse collection, water installation and access for deliveries. If you plan to keep animals, contact the environmental health department.

If it seems difficult to obtain planning permission, ask for the reasons: if these are sensible, try to meet the objections. If not, lobby – first through local councillors and then through the leader of the council or a senior official in the Town Clerk's department. As a last resort, submit a planning appeal – contact the planning department or the Planning Aid Unit at the TCPA.†

The problem may be lack of understanding. Visual presentation of the plans could help: busy officers often do not have the time to sift through detailed descriptions of imaginative wasteland projects. The City Farms Advisory Service at Inter-Action† has films, video tapes and photographs, and can even help to set up a model project of the site for one or two days to show all those concerned what might happen. Friends of the Earth† have a lot of information on gardening projects. These voluntary groups will offer help free of charge if they have the time available.

*As from 1st April 1981.
†See the Appendix for the address.

A licence or lease?

The difference between a licence and a lease is that 'a lease entitles the tenant to exclusive possession for some definite period; but if a person is not to have the exclusive possession of, or sole dominion over the matter [i.e, the property], then his limited right to use and enjoyment is a licence, which confers no estate in the property'.[2]

It is generally much easier to get a licence, for a temporary period. Licences are always restricted to a stated time, have a stated limited purpose and cannot be sold to other people or sub-licensed.

If you do manage to be offered a lease, try to get it for a sufficient period within which to carry out the plans you have. Beware of clauses which require repair, improvement or the expenditure of money. A solicitor can answer any queries, and the following contacts should help: the local citizens advice bureau (find out the address from the library) and The Law Society (see the Appendix for the address).

If you are offered a licence for a council-owned site, you should approach the Council's valuation or estates department. The valuers are responsible for managing land and property held for development within the local authority's boundaries and must ensure that any temporary use of a site does not prejudice its ultimate use. Once a licence has been granted, the valuation officers have to ensure that all the relevant conditions are fulfilled, so that a site is not misused. They are likely to be fairly cautious in the approach to community groups requesting a licence. Despite the insurance policies that licensees have to take out, valuation officers are apprehensive about potential claims on the council's resources and fear that when the council wishes to repossess the site, it might be hard to remove the licensees, especially if the project is popular within the community. Another fear is that the group will not sustain and maintain the project, and the council would then be left to complete it or demolish any buildings

constructed. Therefore preference is often given to well-established groups which have a past record of completing work, such as tenants' associations.

It may sometimes appear that the council is slow in passing the application. If so, a community group would be well advised to make contact with the officers, which would help each side understand the other's operational restraints and speed up the process of getting a licence.

Refusal of a licence

If a licence is refused, a group should approach the local councillor. Ask him to see the borough valuer and find out the reasons for refusal. Alternatively, approach the council committee, either directly or through your councillor, to get their approval in principle. It may be useful to prepare a report for the committee stating what the group wants to do and why, and how much it will cost the council. Many councillors and committees are very sympathetic towards groups trying to carry out community-oriented tasks, and a report should be well received. If the chairman agrees, the committee may accept a delegation to speak on the subject. The precise committee to approach varies from council to council, but look for one which covers the nature of your project (for example, if you are proposing allotments it may be the parks committee, public amenities or public services).

Cost

The cost of the site must be agreed. This can be at a high level because inner city land is frequently valued at a high rate, though land is often temporarily licensed at a low figure.

With a private owner, there is no sanction to persuade him to set a low fee. However, with council ownership, a councillor can help by insisting that the council permit you to have the site for a 'reasonable' sum.

Conditions of planning permission

Having got a lease or a licence, planning permission and agreed the fee, a group must consider the conditions attached to their planning permission. For example, they may be obliged to fence in the site. If it is impossible to meet the conditions, try discussing the matter with your planning department.

Insurance

It is important to take out the widest possible insurance cover, especially in respect of public liability. This will insure groups against claims arising from damage to third parties. The National Playing Fields Association has experience of the type of insurance required by groups and organisations managing children's play and play leadership facilities. Advice about this is available from the Association free of charge (see the Appendix for the address).

Some final words of advice

- Do not rush through the various steps involved in obtaining the land.
- Always put everything in writing and keep copies of all correspondence.

4. Getting Involved – What Community Groups Can Do

Ideas abound on urban wasteland projects for community groups and local authorities.[1] The following give an indication of some of the possibilities.[2]

Allotments

An allotments project is a very good way of using vacant land. In London alone there are 20,000 acres of vacant land which could provide allotment spaces for 323,000 people. Friends of the Earth estimate that even if only half the vacant and derelict sites in London were to be used for food production, 100,000 tons of potatoes or 95,000 tons of cabbages could be grown there.

The demand for allotments is rising, particularly in inner city areas where access to gardens is limited to comparatively few.

A council is legally required to consider allotments under the Smallholdings and Allotments Act 1908. This states that if the bodies responsible for providing allotments (the London boroughs, district councils, the parish meeting in Wales and the community councils) are 'of the opinion that there is a demand for allotments . . . in the borough . . . the council shall provide a sufficient number of allotments to persons . . . resident in the borough . . . and desiring to take the same'. However, the council is not bound to make any provision, since the Act also says: 'On a representation in writing . . . by any registered parliamentary electors or rate payers resident in the borough . . . the Council shall take such representation into consideration.' Hence it is only the council's *opinion* which matters.

5 Community gardening club for the elderly at Inter-Action's City Farm 1, 1977.

Provision of allotments by London local authorities

Inner London borough councils are not legally bound to the 1908 Act (s.55(4) of the Local Government Act 1963). Similarly, the GLC has no specific allotment powers, although it can use vacant land as temporary allotments. However, local authorities are empowered under S.137 of the Local Government Act 1972 to spend up to the product of a 2p rate levy on the provision of services which they are not statutorily obliged to provide. This levy can be used by councils as a useful means of establishing allotments.

Provision of allotments by nationalised industries

Many allotments owned by the British Waterways Board, British Railways, London Transport and the National Coal Board are allocated to their employees. However, it might be possible to negotiate separate access for the general public. As mentioned in chapter 2, statutory undertakers are under a legal obligation in certain areas of the country to register any significant plots of vacant land in their possession, and the Secretary of State is empowered to direct that this land is disposed of on terms directed by him (Local Government, Planning and Land Act 1980).

Acquisition of land

An allotments authority may buy or lease land on which to provide allotments, transfer to allotment-use land it already owns, and may use land earmarked for other purposes temporarily as allotments. With continuing development, temporary allotments might meet all the demands without any permanent appropriation of land.

Management of allotments

Various changes are made to the management of allotments in Schedule 5 of the Local Government, Planning and Land Act 1980. It was proposed to abolish central control on allotment provision and remove the stipulation contained in the 1925 Allotments Act that the Secretary of

State must give consent to the disposal of allotments and ensure 'that adequate provision will be made for allotment holders displaced by the action of the Local Authority or that such provision is unnecessary or not reasonably practicable'. This proposal was dropped in the final version of the Act. However, the Department of the Environment's attitude is indicated by the fact that in 1978 it gave permission to dispose of 250 acres of land suitable for allotments to other uses.

Certain other sections of Allotments Acts have been repealed by the 1980 Act. Section 59 of the Smallholdings and Allotments Act 1908, which obliges the Secretary of State to report annually to Parliament on the state of allotment provision in the country, is repealed. The Department of the Environment claims that as this law has been ignored since 1939 it can now be abolished, which, as Friends of the Earth point out, will hinder both Parliamentary and public accountability for the provision of allotments.

Local authorities are no longer required to keep separate allotments accounts (following the repeal of s.32(2) of the Smallholdings and Allotments Act 1908). Nor are they now required to publish an annual allotments account, or seek the permission of the Secretary of State to transfer allotment funds to other purposes, as laid down in s.54(1) and (2) of the Smallholdings and Allotments Act 1908. This means that it is now harder to get public access to information about allotments. The repeal of s.13 of the Allotments Act 1925, which empowers the Secretary of State to specify the content of local authorities' annual reports to the Minister, likewise clearly indicates difficulties for those wishing to get hold of an allotment.

However, despite these changes in legislation, the basic obligation for local authorities to provide allotments still exists, and a waiting list of over 120,000 for allotments in England and Wales shows that the demand is growing. Indeed pressure groups such as Friends of the Earth strongly encourage people to campaign for

changing wasteland into allotments.

Sources of advice and information

Allotments for the Future
339a Sherrard Road
Manor Park, London E12 6UH
Publication: Newsletter

Friends of the Earth
9 Poland Street, London W1V 3DG
Tel: 01-434 1684
Publications: Riley, Peter, *Economic Growth: the allotments campaign guide,* 1979; *Waste Not Want Not: local opportunities for action on food* (available from Lambeth Friends of the Earth)

Inter-Action
Talacre Open Space
15 Wilkin Street, London NW5 3NG
Tel: 01-485 0881

London Association of Recreational Gardeners
45 The Ridgeway
Keston, Harrow, Middlesex
Tel: 01-907 2040
Publication: *The Recreation Gardener* (monthly journal)

National Society of Allotment and Leisure Gardeners Ltd
22 High Street, Flitwick
Bedfordshire MK45 1DT
Tel: 05257 2361

Further information
Garner, J. F., *The Law of Allotments,* Shaw & Sons Ltd, 1978

16 Mudchute Farm on the Isle of Dogs in London's Docklands.

City Farms

A city farm is a comparatively new and exciting idea for making use of urban vacant land. The first city farm was set up by Inter-Action, a community arts and resources organisation, in Kentish Town, London.

What is a city farm?

City farms are small-scale (from one-third to three acres) agricultural and horticultural projects, on inner city land which would otherwise be vacant. The 'farms' are totally different from real farms since they are not concerned with the commercial production of foods and crops, but provide the means for city people – both adults and children – to experience working with animals and growing crops, and to *manage the project themselves*. This fulfils a social and educational need, rather than a conventional economic need.

City Farm 1

Although there are currently city farms scattered throughout the country, for example in London, Bristol,* Newcastle, Birmingham, Liverpool, Nottingham and Sunderland, the original City Farm 1 serves as a useful model for subsequent experiments. Built on reclaimed land and former British Rail allotments land, it incorporated a wide range of projects which provided for a large spectrum of the community, including:

A small garden for the elderly and kitchen gardens for families.

---

* An interesting project which encompasses a wide variety of wasteland schemes including allotments, the Windmill Hill City Farm and building a medieval barn from disused Dutch elm timber is the Bristol City Land Use Project (now known as the Green Cure Trust), 19 Gordon Road, Clifton, Bristol BS8 1AW. The Project has published a book describing some of its activities, *Sleeping Beauty in the Wood,* which is available from the same address.

Sheep, pigs, horses, chickens and goats which were reared by the local children.

An indoor riding school (created by renovating a derelict timber storage shed).

Stables, tack room, hay shed, store room and a caretaker's flat.

17 Local residents at Inter-Action's City Farm 1, 1977.

The farm catered for every age group: school children learned how to take care of animals; riding lessons for the handicapped took place at the weekends and children from the local estate met after school to ride; parents and members of the Community Garden Club for the elderly worked on the allotments. Inter-Action points out the very small amount of vandalism on the farm – largely because the creation and establishment of the project involved so many local people.

Setting up a city farm

Inter-Action has a City Farms Advisory Service (set up in 1976) which will advise groups about funding and provide starter money. It currently has helped twenty groups' medium and long-term projects. The Service advises that at the initial stage there should be a feasibility study and public consultation, perhaps incorporating a slide show, exhibitions and meetings in places such as shopping centres. The rest of the process – getting the land released, working with planners, etc. – is described in this book. Groups needing advice can contact the Planning Aid Unit at the TCPA – or the City Farms Advisory Service.

Finally, city farms can provide a potentially valuable way of utilising existing resources in the neighbourhood, for example, by using:

- local unemployed people engaged from Manpower Services Commission Special Programmes;
- many locally produced waste products, such as left over produce from local grocers or markets, unwanted sand, top soil and timber;
- the skills and energy of local people which are channelled into a low cost project of direct benefit to the community.

Sources of advice and information

Inter-Action City Farms Advisory Service
15 Wilkin Street, London NW5 3NG
Tel: 01-485 0881
Publications: *Where to Find City Farms in Britain* gives addresses of existing city farms; *City Farms News* (three times a year)

Town and Country Planning Association
Planning Aid Unit
17 Carlton House Terrace
London SW1Y 5AS
Tel: 01-930 8903/4/5
Publications: The TCPA's Community Technical Aid Centre has produced a series of leaflets on 'Tackling Inner City Problems', which include

Ideas Sheets on: 'General Improvements on Wasteland Sites', 'Nature Areas from Wasteland Sites', and 'City Farms on Wasteland Sites'

Further information
Gordon, David, 'Towards an Urban Farm', The Soil Association, March 1978
Knights, Kay, 'City Farms', *Association of Agriculture Journal,* Autumn 1977
Oldfield, Tony, 'Dockland Farm', *Water Space,* No. 13, Spring 1978

Community Gardens

'Community garden' is a rather loosely used term to cover projects which actively involve residents and community groups in the design, planting and maintenance of some open space. These are often short-term projects.

Such gardens are not intended to enter into competition with other schemes. Indeed, the quality of design and amenities provided by a community garden largely depends on the enthusiasm, energy and ideas of the group working on the project, their funding assistance and the support of the local authority which grants a licence for the garden.

Setting up a community garden
Since these gardens vary in size and since local authority support for community initiatives varies, the problems involved in setting up a community garden differ greatly. The best documented initiative is described below.

Meanwhile Gardens
Meanwhile Gardens is a garden in Paddington, West London, situated between the canal, the railway line and the motorway. Jamie McCullough, in his book *Meanwhile Gardens,* charts its progress from a strip of wasteland

18 Community gardens at the Abercromby Farm Project in Liverpool.

19 Allens Gardens, Tower Hamlets, 1980.
In the midst of a densely occupied residential area, Allens Gardens is a breath of fresh air. At present it is best described as a derelict park planted with mature specimen trees and overgrown bushes, and full of character. It once belonged to a family trust that built flats in the 1870s around two sides of a triangle closed by a railway cutting, and was an amenity to be enjoyed by all. Now privately owned, the land is a subject of a planning application for more residential development. A local action group is fighting to preserve this extraordinary private park and open it for use by residents.

covered with broken concrete, tangled iron, fly-tipped wreckage and corrugated iron, to a park with trees, grass, bicycle and skateboard tracks and a theatre – all created by local residents with the help of Manpower Services Commission labour, funding from various grant-giving bodies and materials and expertise voluntarily donated.

Improvements
Community gardens may incorporate a range of improvements and amenities. The following are a sample list of things that can be done:
● clear rubbish, improve fencing (to prevent tipping) and grass over the land with soil, seed and fertilizer followed by harrowing. Contact the parks department of the local council;
● establish an 'ecological area', perhaps in or near a school.[3] A local urban studies centre may also give advice and information.* Contact your local council or the Education Unit of the TCPA for further details;
● set paving, footpaths and public seats. Contact the highways department;
● paint murals to brighten cleared sites. Contact the highways or housing departments.

*Details of urban studies centres are contained in the *Bullet. of Environmental Education,* available from the TCPA.

20 Mural in Washington New Town, 1978.
The painting, around a circular play space, represents 101 ways to kill a dragon – based on the local legend about the Lampton worm. The artists were local children.

Sources of advice and information

British Trust for Conservation Volunteers
10-14 Duke Street
Reading, Berkshire RG1 4RU
Tel: 0734 596171

Committee for Environmental Conservation
(CoEnCo) Youth Unit
Zoological Gardens, London NW1 4RY
Tel: 01-722 7111

National Federation of Community Organisations
26 Bedford Square, London WC1B 3HU
Tel: 01-636 4066

Nature Conservancy Council
19 Belgrave Square, London SW1X 8PY
Tel: 01-235 3241

William Curtis Ecological Park
16 Vine Lane, Tooley Street
Bermondsey, London SE1 2JQ
Tel: 01-403 2078

Further information
McCullough, Jamie, *Meanwhile Gardens,* 1978.
Available from the Calouste Gulbenkian
Foundation, 98 Portland Place, London W1N 4ET.
Tel: 01-636 5313
'Purpose in the park', *Public Service and Local
Government;* Vol 8, August/Sept 1978, pp 28-32

21 Mural self-portrait at Mudchute City Farm, 1979.

Adventure Playgrounds

Many adventure playgrounds have been started and run by groups of parents and community groups in conjunction with a local authority, on vacant land awaiting redevelopment. Some councils, such as Hammersmith in London, have used vacant land as an opportunity to provide temporary or long-term adventure playgrounds during school summer holidays.

This type of play area is inexpensive, since many of the structures can be built from scrap materials. The main necessities are ropes, tyres, an unending supply of wood, tools and nails. However, it is also necessary to have full-time playworkers at adventure playgrounds – a cost normally borne by the local authority.

The site itself should be fenced off; to protect the equipment, prevent rubbish heaping, give a sense of security to the children and avoid any visual offence to neighbours. The playground should have good access, for lorries to deliver materials and for the children to reach it safely.

Management and finance

The National Playing Fields Association advise that an

> effective management committee, with many of its members drawn from the immediate neighbourhood, is essential. Representatives of the local authority and other interested bodies could also be invited to join. Local authorities, although assuming financial responsibility, are advised to run the

2 Adventure playground, Battersea Park, 1979.
One of many such purpose-built adventure playgrounds, this typifies what can be done with small areas of unused land in localities lacking facilities for children. Essentially temporary in nature, the playgrounds make excellent use of urban sites that have been left over, ignored or remain unplanned. Sadly, councils seem to be less and less prepared to pay for such sites, preferring a dangerous vacant lot to an active, useful and imaginative feature in the neighbourhood.

playgrounds by means of management
committees. The playleader is responsible to
the committee, which will assist him or her in
obtaining materials and in contacts with all
the appropriate departments of the local
authority . . . it is essential that a playleader
receives support from the committee.
Local authorities are usually the only
organisation able to bear the financial
responsibility for the major part of the annual
outgoings such as salaries, main services and
general upkeep. Providing certain essential
conditions are fulfilled, the National Playing
Fields Association can make a grant-in-aid to the
first year's salary of a playleader and to initial
capital costs and equipment. There will always
be a need for expenditure on 'extras', which will
not be met from official sources, so the local
community should be involved from the start in
fund-raising activities. This will lead to a greater
interest in the playground and a feeling of
responsibility for it.

Sources of advice and information
Child's Play
Francis House, Francis Street
London SW1P 1DE
Tel: 01-828 7364

Fair Play for Children
248 Kentish Town Road
London NW5 2AB
Tel: 01-485 0809

National Children's Bureau
8 Wakley Street, London EC1V 7QE
Tel: 01-278 9441

National Playing Fields Association
25 Ovington Square, London SW3 1LQ
Tel: 01-584 6445

Pre-School Playgroups Association
Alford House, Aveline Street
London SW11 5DH
Tel: 01-582 8871

5. Creating Employment from Wasteland Projects

Employment and urban wasteland

So far this book has looked at how urban wasteland is a resource in physical, social and environmental terms. It also has other assets, particularly in relation to employment.[1]

The White Paper *Policy for the Inner Cities* (June 1979) states: 'The highest proportion of unskilled and semi-skilled people in the inner areas points to the need for some change in manpower policies to meet the employment and training needs of inner area residents.' One way of creating employment is by using both local unemployed manpower resources and local vacant land resources.

Creating employment

There is great employment potential in many wasteland schemes, especially 'socially useful' projects. They can be of benefit to the environment and therefore to the local community and, in particular, train young people to acquire skills which will help them find employment in the longer term. These ideas are already being examined by educationalists, environmentalists and trade unionists. For example, John Ewan suggested the creation of 'community industry' for young unemployed people* — work which encompasses both environmental improvement and a social element such as housing renovation or health care.[2] Such schemes would also enable the maximum participation of the young workers.

Ewan's ideas formed the basis of the government's 'community industry' schemes.

23 Community Industry, Wandsworth, 1978.
Unemployed local kids learn a trade under the supervision of an ex-bricklayer, and create a sitting-out area on a small patch of vacant land in Battersea. The scheme, a national one, has provided facilities of all kinds on land that no one seemed to think was useable.

Community projects can provide employment, particularly through the Youth Opportunities Programme (YOP) and the Community Enterprise Programme (CEP). It is important to ensure that schemes run under the Manpower Services Commission's (MSC) Special Programmes train youngsters in a skill, so that they do not just go back to the dole queue after six months or a year. Projects which could provide this include: doing urban ecological or geological surveys when evaluating sites; surveying the extent of wasteland within a locality; building on a site (in Meanwhile Gardens in West London people were employed to build a theatre and skateboard and bicycle tracks), and horticultural and agricultural work, for example on an urban farm.

Perhaps one of the most exciting 'employment from wasteland' schemes is the Rhondda Enterprises workshop in Porth, Rhondda Valley. Here a disused building, which was formerly a school and council depot, has been converted into a training workshop for young people, using money from Urban Aid and the MSC STEP scheme. The workshop aims to produce goods that are needed locally (e.g. television stands for local schools) while training young people in skills demanded by Rhondda industries; both goods and skills in demand have been identified in preliminary surveys. Rhondda Enterprises' future plans are ambitious: they hope to assist those trained in the Porth workshop in setting up smaller workshops in the disused chapels and factories throughout the Rhondda. If successful, Rhondda could offer a pattern of revitalisation that community groups in declining areas can follow. For further details contact: *Rhondda Enterprises, Pemrhiwgwynt Road, Porth, Rhondda, Mid-Glamorgan CF39 9UB. Tel: 044 361 2312/6118.*

Community groups do find that there are many problems connected with MSC temporary employment schemes. The following are examples.
● The low wages offered under the CEP programme are a key problem which is accentuated if skilled craftsmen are needed who could get higher wages elsewhere. This may mean that a group has to recruit non-MSC funded labour, which becomes very expensive.

● At present, the wages paid under YOP may appear low, which again makes it difficult to recruit people, unless there is an extremely high level of unemployment in the area.

● For both the YOP and STEP programmes, supervisors usually must come from the unemployment register. This may well prove a problem if the group is trying to recruit skilled people, especially in London.

24 Young people hauling timber to build a medieval-style barn – part of the Bristol City Land Use Project (now known as Green Cure Trust).

- MSC tries to hire four trainees for every supervisory craftsman. Jamie McCullough in his book *Meanwhile Gardens*[3] advises that a group try to keep this ratio down to 1:2, since this is the best way of training people. He also advises limiting the numbers employed to eight, since any more could create an unstable group.

- There might be a problem with site discipline, since hiring of YOP trainees depends on referrals from the careers service. Firing should be carried out in conjunction with MSC. Under CEP, hiring must be carried out with the approval of MSC.

MSC will not pay anyone within a community group or allow very much towards the cost of materials, so that the group has to continue fund raising.

There may be problems with unions if people are recruited via MSC; all MSC Job Creation programmes should be worked out in consultation with the unions.

Although none of the problems outlined above are insurmountable, they should be taken into account before a group embarks on projects which provide employment. It may take time, patience and energy to employ people on wasteland or vacant land properties but the potential benefits, both economic and social, are great.

Sources of advice and information

Centre for Alternative Industrial and
Technological Systems
North East London Polytechnic
Longbridge Road, Barking
Essex RM8 2BS
Tel: 01-590 7722

The Local Enterprise Advisory Project has been established to assist groups in areas of high unemployment in the west of Scotland and to investigate, design and prepare local schemes to provide long-term viable employment. Contact John Pearce at:
Local Government Unit
Paisley College of Technology
High Street, Paisley, Renfrewshire
Scotland
Publication: Pearce, John, *Can We Make Jobs: a local community based approach to industrial development,* available from the Local Government Unit of the Paisley College of Technology

Manpower Services Commission
Selkirk House, 166 High Holborn
London WC1V 6PF
Tel: 01-836 1213

Wasteland Forum
NCVO
26 Bedford Square
London WC1B 3HU
Tel: 01-636 4066

6. Fund Raising

Fund raising is never easy: it requires patience, tact, imagination and contacts. However, many bodies give grants to voluntary organisations, so persevere!

Government grants

As mentioned on p. 13, there are various government grants available for local authority and voluntary organisations' projects on inner city wasteland.

The following is a summary of the main sources of government financial aid in England. For further details contact the *DOE, 2 Marsham Street, London SW1P 3EB. Tel: 01-212 3434.*

Urban aid
As mentioned in chapter 2, funds are available for both local authority and voluntary sector projects under the Urban Programme. Local authorities with inner city partnership or programme authority status receive block allocations of funds from the DOE in respect of their Inner Area Programmes. Other authorities with evidence of 'special social need' can apply annually in response to the DOE Circular for the Traditional Urban Programme for grants for capital and non-capital projects run by themselves or voluntary organisations.

Environmental improvement grants
Environmental improvement grants are available for projects sponsored by local authorities and community groups in both General Improvement Areas and Housing Action Areas. Environmental improvement projects may include tree planting, providing play spaces, grassed or paved areas and pedestrian ways.

Conservation grants
Conservation Areas qualify for grants and loans for environmental improvements from the Historic Buildings Council. Such grants are available to voluntary organisations, local authorities, housing associations and private owners. Grants are mainly given for work to buildings but they may also cover a wide range of environmental improvements such as landscaping and the restoration of traditional paving. For further details contact the *Historic Buildings Council for England, 25 Saville Row, London W1X 1AA. Tel: 01-734 6010.*

Derelict land grants
Derelict land grants are available to local authorities and private individuals for purposes connected with the acquisition, clearance and reclamation of derelict land (see chapter 2).

Manpower Services Commission
It may be possible to employ people to work on inner city wasteland projects through CEP and YOP projects, which are funded by MSC. Further information is available from the Commission, *Selkirk House, 166 High Holborn, London WC1V 6PF. Tel: 01-836 1213.*

Local authorities

Local authorities may decide to give financial assistance to projects run by community groups. Some authorities already have a policy of granting money for schemes on wasteland: the GLC has allocated a small sum of money for voluntary projects on wasteland in GLC areas. Contact the *Transportation and Development Department of the GLC (County Hall, London SE1 7PB. Tel: 01-633 7160)* or your district or county council.

Trusts and foundations

There are a number of trusts and foundations which will give financial assistance to projects run by community groups. These include the Rowntrees Social Services Trust, the Gulbenkian Foundation and the Sainsbury Trusts. The best source of information about these is the *Directory of Grant-Making Trusts,* published by the *Charities Aid Foundation, 48 Pembury Road, Tonbridge, Kent TN9 2JD. Tel: 0732 356323.*

Some major companies may sponsor groups' projects: it could be worthwhile writing to companies such as Shell and Rank Xerox. Large local firms or local enterprise trusts may also help fund projects and help provide materials such as topsoil or local tools.

Environmental organisations

There are a number of environmental organisations that will give grants, especially if the projects incorporate environmental improvements. Get in touch with the following for details:

Countryside Commission
John Dower House
Crescent Place, Cheltenham
Gloucestershire GL50 3RA
Tel: 0242 21381

Civic Trust
17 Carlton House Terrace
London SW1Y 5AW
Tel: 01-930 0914

National Playing Fields Association
25 Ovington Square, London SW3 1LQ
Tel: 01-584 6445

The Prince of Wales Committee
Sophia Gardens Lodge, Cardiff CF1 9LJ
Tel: 0222 373600

Queen's Silver Jubilee Trust
8 Buckingham Street, London WC2N 6BU
Tel: 01-930 9811

Sports Council
70 Brompton Road, London SW3 1EX
Tel: 01-589 3411

Further information
NCVO publishes under its Bedford Square Press imprint a useful reference book, *Sources of Statutory Money: a guide for voluntary organisations* (1980).

Example of funding for Meanwhile Gardens, London W10

Access	£ 100
Greater London Arts Association	£ 400
J.G. Promotions – Skateboard Championship proceeds	£ 4
Edward Harvist Trust	£ 1,500
Community Relations Council	£ 850
Paddington Charitable Estates	£ 1,000
Cash donation	£ 15
Whitbread & Co	£ 50
BBC Facility Fee	£ 15
Hayward Foundation	£ 2,500
Job Creation Programme	£15,186

Silver Jubilee Committee	Salary for Jamie McCullough for 9 months
Taylor Woodrow	Site hut
Meeres Bros	4 months free usage of bulldozer
Amery Roadstone	Concrete to do ¼ of bicycle track
Paddington Print Shop	Printing at cost
Jones Reinforcement	Reinforcement for skateboard track
Dunlop	14 pairs of wellingtons
E. McBean & Co	Waterproof garments
W. W. Johnson	Grass seed at slightly below cost
Kensal Play Association	Workshop

Source: *The Use of Unused Land for Community Purposes,* Report by a Working Party of the Environmental Committee for the London Celebrations for the Queen's Silver Jubilee (1977).

Conclusion

This book has shown how both community groups and local authorities can make the most of urban wasteland, although it may take time, patience and perseverance.

Vested control over how inner city land is used, until recently, has lain solely in the hands of local authorities, statutory undertakers and private owners. But, as this book demonstrates, community groups can and do acquire both the confidence and skills to put urban wasteland to a host of imaginative uses. What it takes is a sympathetic local authority, a group's energy, commitment and fund-raising ability, and lastly, technical assistance from both professional and voluntary bodies.

By becoming involved in wasteland projects, residents of a neighbourhood can gain increased confidence to take part in many other local environmental activities. Indeed, people only begin to have control over their urban environment when they decide to take direct action themselves.

'For fulfilment there must be a resorbtion of government into the body of the community. How? By cultivating the habit of direct action instead of waiting upon representative agencies.' Patrick Geddes, 'What to do' – unpublished, 1912

Notes

1. Where is Urban Wasteland and Why Does It Exist?
1 Cantell, T., *Urban Wasteland*, Civic Trust, October 1977
2 *Policy for the Inner Cities*, Cmnd 6845, HMSO, 1977
3 Jones, C., *Urban Deprivation and the Inner City*, Croom Helm, 1979
4 Foreman-Peck, J. S. and Griapisos, A. J., *Inner City Problems and Inner City Policies*, Regional Studies, Vol 11, No 6, 1977
5 Howard, E., *Garden Cities of Tomorrow*, Faber, 1902
6 Cantell, T., op.cit.
7 *Profits Against Housing*, Community Development Project, 1976
8 *Trends in Housing and Construction*, National Building Agency, 1976
9 'Vacant urban land and its planning implications', unpublished M Phil thesis, Bartlett School of Architecture, 1977
0 *Strategic Issues for Strathclyde*, Strathclyde Regional Council Draft Survey Report, 1976
1 Colenutt, R., 'Are inner city land values a problem?', *Architects Journal*, 5 July 1978
2 *Land Values and Planning in the Inner Areas*, Final Report of the RTPI, 1979

. Government and Local Authority Action on Vacant Inner City Land
1 'Vacant land', Department of the Environment, 1AS/C1/11, 1976. Available from HMSO
2 1978 map of Vacant and Potentially Vacant Sites is available from the London Borough of Southwark, Borough Development Department, 30-32 Peckham Road, London SE5 8QP
3 The Lambeth Survey of Vacant Sites is available from the London Borough of Lambeth, Planning Department, 9-15 New Park Road, London SW2 4DU
4 'Vacant land in Tower Hamlets', October 1978, is available from the London Borough of Tower Hamlets, Planning Department, Town Hall, Bow Road, London E3 2SE
5 'Halton anti-vandalism campaign', Final Report, April 1976. Available from Halton Borough Council, Municipal Building, Kingsway, Widnes, Cheshire WA8 7QF

Voluntary Action on Wasteland
1 See Hall, C., *How to Run a Pressure Group*, Dent, 1974
2 Redman, J. H., *The Law of Landlord and Tenant*, Butterworth, 8th edn, 1924

4. Getting Involved – What Community Groups Can Do
1 One possible source of ideas is Matthews, R. J., *Short Term Use of Vacant Land*, GLC, 1978
2 A useful book is Miller, T., *Self-Help in the Environment: a handbook for parish councils, voluntary services and others*, Nottinghamshire Association for Local Councils, 1976
3 See Simonon, L., *Making Playgrounds*, Community Service Volunteers, 1979

5. Creating Employment from Wasteland Projects
1 Bramley, G., Stewart, M., and Underwood, J., *Local Economic Initiatives*, School for Advanced Urban Studies, 1978
2 Ewan, John, 'A community work scheme for unemployed young people', *Bulletin of Environmental Education*, April 1972. *The Bulletin of Environmental Education* is available from the TCPA.
3 McCullough, J., *Meanwhile Gardens*, 1978. Available from the Calouste Gulbenkian Foundation, 98 Portland Place, London W1N 4ET

Further Reading

'Britain's idle acres' by T. Cantell in *Built Environment,* Vol 3, No 3, September 1972

Derelict Land: origins and prospects of a land-use problem by K. L. Wallwork, David and Charles, 1974

Development of Publicly Owned Urban Land. Available from the Association of Metropolitan Authorities, 36 Old Queen Street, London SW1H 9JE

The Endless Village by W. G. Teagle, Nature Conservancy Council, 1978. Available from HMSO

Extent and Development of Derelict Land in England in the 1970s by K. L. Wallwork, Royal Town Planning Institute, 1976

Fight Blight by C. McKean, Kaye and Ward, 1977
'How much vacant land?' by J. W. Burrows, *Architects Journal,* Vol 165, No 20, 1977

Inner Cities of Tomorrow. Policy statement by the TCPA, March 1977. Available from the TCPA, 17 Carlton House Terrace, London SW1Y 5AS

Land-use Perspectives, Land Decade Educational Council, 1979

Vacant Land in Liverpool, Liverpool Council for Voluntary Service, 1977

Wasteland Bulletin, a quarterly publication produced by the Wasteland Forum, NCVO, 26 Bedford Square, London WC1B 3HU. The Wasteland Forum aims to encourage the use of urban wasteland by voluntary and community groups and it provides a wide range of advisory services to groups about wasteland utilisation projects.

Appendix: Useful addresses*

Allotments for the Future, 339a Sherrard Road, Manor Park, London E12 6UH

British Trust for Conservation Volunteers, 10-14 Duke Street, Reading, Berkshire RG1 4RU. Tel: 0734 596171

Child's Play, Francis House, Francis Street, London SW1P 1DE. Tel: 01-828 7364

Civic Trust, 17 Carlton House Terrace, London SW1Y 5AW. Tel: 01-930 0914

Committee for Environmental Conservation (CoEnCo) Youth Unit, Zoological Gardens, London NW1 4RY. Tel: 01-722 7111

Community Service Volunteers, 237 Pentonville Road, London N1 9NJ. Tel: 01-278 6601

Community Task Force, Lowthian House, Market Street, Preston, Lancs. Tel: 0772 51878

COMTECHSA (Community Technical Services Agency), Westminster Chambers, 3 Crosshall Street, Liverpool L16 0Q

Countryside Commission, John Dower House, Crescent Place, Cheltenham, Glos. GL50 3RA. Tel: 0242 21381

Department of the Environment, 2 Marsham Street, London SW1P 3EB. Tel: 01-212 3434

East End Wildlife Group, 222 Cable Street, London E1 0BL. Tel: 01-791 0400

Environmental Resource Centre, Old Broughton School, McDonald Road, Edinburgh EH7 4ID. Tel: 031 557 2135

Fair Play for Children, 248 Kentish Town Road, London NW5 2AB. Tel: 01-485 0809

*Including some not mentioned in the text.

Friends of the Earth, 9 Poland Street, London W1V 3DG. Tel: 01-434 1684

Green Cure Trust, 19 Gordon Road, Clifton, Bristol BS8 1AW. Tel: 0272 33217

HM Land Registry, 32 Lincoln's Inn Fields, London WC2A 3PH. Tel: 01-405 3488

Historic Buildings Council for England, 25 Saville Row, London W1X 1AA. Tel: 01-734 6010

Impact, Civic Trust North West, Environmental Institute, Greaves School, Bolton Road, Swinton, Manchester M27 2UX

Inter-Action, Talacre Open Space, 15 Wilkin Street, London NW5 3NG. Tel: 01-485 0881

Land Decade, c/o Land Council, 9 Queen Anne's Gate, London SW1H 9BU. Tel: 01-222 4333

The Law Society, 113 Chancery Lane, London WC2A 1PL. Tel: 01-242 1222

London Association of Recreational Gardeners, 45 The Ridgeway, Keston, Harrow, Middx. Tel: 01-907 2040

Manpower Services Commission, Selkirk House, 166 High Holborn, London WC1V 6PF. Tel: 01-836 1213

National Children's Bureau, 8 Wakely Street, London EC1V 7QE. Tel: 01-278 9441

National Council for Voluntary Organisations, 26 Bedford Square, London WC1B 3HU. Tel: 01-636 4066

National Federation of Community Organisations, 26 Bedford Square, London WC1B 3HU. Tel: 01-636 4066

National Playing Fields Association, 25 Ovington Square, London SW3 1LQ. Tel: 01-584 6445

National Society of Allotment and Leisure Gardeners, 22 High Street, Flitwick, Bedford MK45 1DT. Tel: 05257 2361

Nature Conservancy Council, 19 Belgrave Square, London SW1X 8PY. Tel: 01-235 3241

Nature Conservancy Council for Scotland, 12 Hope Terrace, Edinburgh EH9 2AS. Tel: 031 447 4784

Pre-School Playgroups Association, Alford House, Aveline Street, London SE11 5DH. Tel: 01-582 8871

The Prince of Wales Committee, Sophia Gardens Lodge, Cardiff CF1 9LJ. Tel: 0222 373600

Royal Society for the Promotion of Nature Conservation (RSPNC), 22 The Green, Nettleham, Lincoln, Lincs LN2 2NR. Tel: 0522 52351

Royal Town Planning Institute, 26 Portland Place, London W1N 4BE. Tel: 01-636 9017

Rural Preservation Association, The Old Police Station, Lark Lane, Liverpool 17. Tel: 051 728 7011

Society for Horticultural Therapy, 52 Catherine Street, Frome, Somerset BA11 1DA. Tel: 0373 4782

Town and Country Planning Association, Planning Aid Unit, 17 Carlton House Terrace, London SW1Y 5AS. Tel: 01-930 8903/4/5

Town Teacher, 25 Queen Street, Newcastle NE1 3UG. Tel: 0632 29541

Wasteland Forum, NCVO, 26 Bedford Square, London WC1B 3HU. Tel: 01-636 4066

William Curtis Ecological Park, 16 Vine Lane, Tooley Street, Bermondsey, London SE1 2JQ. Tel: 01-403 2078

Youthaid, 57 Chalton Street, London NW1 1HY

Youth Environmental Action, 173 Archway Road, London N6 5BL. Tel: 01-348 3030

also available from the Bedford Square Press:

Co-operatives and Community: the theory and practice of producer co-operatives
Going Local: neighbourhood social services (NCVO Occasional Paper 1)
Making Work: some examples of Job Creation schemes
Public Participation in Britain: a classified bibliography
Route Causes: a guide to participation in public transport plans
Sources of Statutory Money: a guide for voluntary organisations
Tribunal Representation: the role of advice and advocacy services
Voluntary Organisations: an NCVO directory 1982/83
Work and the Community: a report on MSC Special Programmes for the unemployed

Available from NCVO:

The Urban Programme: Guidance for voluntary organisation (Inner Cities Unit)
Wasteland Bulletin (Wasteland Forum)